Family Name

_____

Date

_____

Our Family Tree

Roots that run deep yield a bounty of love

Barbara Briggs Morrow

new seasons™

a division of Publications International, Ltd.

Barbara Briggs Morrow is a contributing editor for *Midwest Living* magazine and veteran writer whose work has appeared in *Cosmopolitan, Christian Science Monitor,* and the *Des Moines Register.* Her previous books include *American Country Sampler, The Gift of Friendship, A Sister's Memories,* and *Grandparents' Memories.*

Interior Illustrations by Anita C. Nelson.

Louis Weber, C.E.O.
Publications International, Ltd.
7373 North Cicero Avenue
Lincolnwood, Illinois 60712

Manufactured in China.

8 7 6 5 4 3 2 1

new seasons
TM
a division of Publications International, Ltd.

Contents

Climbing the Family Tree

There was a time when families had little need to search for their origins. You knew where you came from, because generation after generation of your family had lived in the same town. Births and deaths were recorded faithfully in the family Bible, and stories passed from old to young during long winter evenings around the hearth. Youngsters committed histories and tales to memory for fun, so they were able to pass the information on when their turns came. Any information that eluded this traditional exchange could be recovered easily enough. Research was a simple matter of chatting with great-grandmother or strolling to the village hall or church to check family records there.

Family history provided a sort of foundation on which each generation could build. Knowing that your people had always been farmers or fishermen or merchants helped you understand yourself. Tales of ancestors' bravery, triumphs, and sacrifices were sources of pride, as well as examples to be followed. Past family trials and challenges served as cautions for the current generation and warnings to be handed down.

Eventually, migrations strained—and sometimes broke—these generations-old ties to a family's past. Modern life and technology severed many of the links that remained. Immigrants left behind not only the Old Country, but also, in many cases, older family members not able to make the difficult journey. Family records probably stayed with the grandparents, and, despite the best of intentions, memories once carefully preserved eventually faded. Those who lugged massive old Bibles or other records to their new homeland sometimes lost them to the elements or were forced to discard them at difficult points in their journeys. Many records that survived became puzzles to Americanized descendants. Notations in a language foreign to the current generation and place-names long ago deleted from maps remained as family mysteries.

Some people might wonder why a family's history matters. All sorts of families with no visible roots flourish in communities that seem to have sprouted whole from nowhere. The melting pot long ago blended immigrant strains so effectively that they seem almost impossible to identify. Does individual history matter anyway when information is exploding faster than school can teach it? In a world where people and things move so fast, the foundations that families once built so carefully hardly seem worth the trouble. Besides, starting all over has practically become an American tradition.

But, for some of us, the present just isn't enough, and what we build ourselves can't replace that deep-rooted family foundation. This conviction may come all at once, or one moment at time. Sorting through the storage room, perhaps, you find an old trunk full of photos, with nameless faces staring at the camera. You wish you knew who they were, and their forthright stares seem to say that you should; you're sure these people have interesting stories to tell. Or maybe one day, a school project sends a child home asking questions. Half-remembered conversations from long ago leave you punctuating your answers with "maybe" and "I'm not sure, but…" "The teacher says we

can't write it down unless we know for sure," the child protests.

You realize you want to know more about your family and your background. You don't feel a need to be absolutely sure of every fact or to track down obscure details, but you need a feeling for your origins and your family's past. It's as if you had been standing in the shade of a towering tree without really thinking about it. Then, you look up and appreciate the tree, thinking how pleasant it would be to climb to at least the lower branches. Without some kind of help—a ladder or even just a boost—you decide it's just too difficult.

Climbing your family tree can seem just as impossible. That's where this book comes in. The introduction to each section will help trigger your thoughts, and

fill-in-the-blank questions will gently guide your search. Recording what you find offers just the "leg-up" that other family members or succeeding generations may need when they want to know more about their roots. The sections needn't be filled out in a certain order; tackle the questions first that interest you most or that you know the most about.

The best place to start, naturally, is at home. Gather and review family records. These can be as official as the family Bible and marriage and birth certificates or as informal as old letters and snapshots. It's a great opportunity to page through all those photo albums and get out the old letters and postcards gathering dust in the storage room.

Call on other family members to search their attics and storerooms. Often, the relatives with the most to share are the happiest to contribute. It's a relief when someone finally shows an interest in

papers, photos, and other family memorabilia with which they have been entrusted. Be sure to ask the person to write down any information they can about the materials, or be prepared to take notes. Perhaps, depending on the volume of information, several meetings are in order.

Next, talk to other family members about what you've discovered, and ask about portions of the family history that you may not be aware of. This book makes a good springboard for those conversations. You may be surprised, once people start talking, just how much they know. Bits and pieces supplied by different family members come together like the pieces of a jigsaw puzzle. The resulting facts and stories will no doubt surprise and delight everyone.

Elderly people often enjoy sharing their recollections and memorabilia. If you and your source are both comfortable with using a little technology, a tape recorder or even a video camera can be an invaluable tool in these meetings.

Also, strike up a correspondence with family members who live far away. Different bits of a family's history may filter through separated family branches. You may want to avoid sharing original records, photographs, or other memorabilia by mail, but photocopies work just as well for many purposes. Then, offer to pay for reproductions of photographs that you'd like to keep or frame.

If you decide that you want to dig deeper, your local library is a good place to start. Look for listings of "how-to" publications as well as contact information for local genealogical societies. Check your local courthouse for official documents such as deeds, wills, and marriage records, or plan a trip to an area where your family once lived and visit the courthouse and any genealogical societies there. These dry documents and listings of names and numbers can be keys to family stories—the good fortune that allowed a land purchase or the will that reveals a family feud.

State libraries and archives hold more records, including some census and military information. The National Archives in Washington, D.C., maintains old census records, ship and passenger arrival lists, and much more. Twelve regional archives are also information sources. If you're wondering about when and how your family arrived in this country, these records may hold the answer. Be aware that name spellings sometimes changed on arrival.

The Genealogical Society of Utah's Family History Library in Salt Lake City is one of the most comprehensive information sources available, with thousands of birth, death, marriage, land, tax, and just about every other sort of record you can think of. More than 2,000 family history centers worldwide also help in family research.

Ironically, the technology that some blame for dividing families has become a source for family tree information. With a home computer and a modem, you can access an array of genealogy sites on the worldwide web, including several with tips for beginning researchers. You can also "chat" with other searchers and tap into informational sources around the world.

Wherever your search leads—to the library or just to your own attic—it will soon become clear what was once lost to you and what you stand to regain. The prize isn't just a list of names and dates, but your family—people who in some way made you who you are, people with lessons and legacies for the present, people who deserve to be remembered.

Tracing Our Roots

The search might begin with a desire to know more about names written in fading ink in an old family Bible. Or perhaps it starts with a child's school project. As the search continues, the details of your family's past begin to unfold like a fascinating story, and you can't wait to discover the next chapter.

If there was one incident that made us want to know more about our family, it was _____

_____

_____.

How we started: _____

_____

_____.

Success stories:_____

_____

_____

_____.

Dead-ends and other frustrations:_____

_____

_____

The "find(s)" that mean the most: _____

_____

_____

_____

_____.

Other information about our search: _____

_____

_____

_____

_____

_____

_____

_____

_____

_____

_____

_____

_____.

The Story Begins

Whether you reach back a half-dozen generations or only a couple, knowing more about the people in your family's history teaches you something valuable about yourself. Below, note what you've discovered so far.

The earliest ancestor we've identified is _____

_____.

His or her story: _____

_____

_____

_____

_____.

How we found this information: _____

_____

_____.

Other interesting people or information we've discovered: _____

_____

_____

_____

Place an old family photo here.

_____

_____

_____

_____

_____

_____

_____

_____

_____ .

Family Origins

*It's exciting to find that the family name wasn't forgotten in a faraway town,
even though newer generations may have lost touch with the place.
Records wait to be discovered in an old church or village hall, and you might
even find someone who remembers a story or two about your loved ones.
Below, record information you have about your family's place(s) of origin.*

What we know about the land where our family originated: _____

_____

_____.

What kind of place was it? _____

_____

_____.

What our people did there: _____

_____

_____.

How we discovered the information: _____

_____

_____.

Other notes about our family origins: _____

_____

_____

What's in a Name?

Names hold important clues to a family's history.
They might provide a link to a trade that ancestors plied or to a place
that your family once called home. The spelling may have changed over the years,
but the tie of a family name is never broken.

Our family surname(s) mean _____.

Our name(s) originated_____.

Meanings and origins of other surnames in our family tree: _____

_____

_____

_____.

The following first names have become something of a family tradition: _____

_____

_____

_____.

When the tradition started: _____

_____

_____

_____.

Other information about names in our family: _____

_____

_____

_____

_____

_____

_____

_____

_____

_____

_____

_____

_____

_____

_____

_____

_____

_____

_____

_____.

Making a New Home

Many Americans' family ties reach across the sea. Immigrants who journeyed to a new land and struggled to settle here lived fascinating adventures. Their sagas deserve to be recorded, both as a tribute to their courage and as a reminder of how far we've come.

How our family(s) came to this country:_____
_____
_____.

The hardest part of the journey was probably_____
_____
_____.

The greatest joy came when _____
_____
_____.

The place we'd most like to return to for a visit: _____
_____.

Other family moves and migrations: _____

_____

_____

_____

_____

_____

_____

_____

_____

_____

_____

_____

_____

_____

_____

_____

_____

_____

_____

_____.

Our Grandparents

*Grandparents can offer some of the most accessible links to the past.
Their stories become important chapters in a family's history and a
valuable record for the future. Below, record favorite memories, well-worn tales,
or other memorable details about your grandparents.*

GRANDMOTHERS' PROFILES:

Name:_____.

Place and date of birth:_____.

Interesting facts, traits, or stories: _____

_____

_____

_____.

Name:_____

Place and date of birth: _____.

Interesting facts, traits, or stories: _____

_____

_____

_____

_____.

Name:_____.

Place and date of birth:_____.

Interesting facts, traits, or stories:_____

_____

_____

_____

_____.

Name:_____.

Place and date of birth:_____.

Interesting facts, traits, or stories:_____

_____

_____

_____

_____.

GRANDFATHERS' PROFILES:

Name:_____.

Place and date of birth:_____.

Interesting facts, traits, or stories:_____

_____

_____

_____.

Name:_____.

Place and date of birth:_____.

Interesting facts, traits, or stories:_____

_____

_____

_____

_____.

Name:_____.

Place and date of birth:_____.

Interesting facts, traits, or stories:_____

_____

_____

_____

_____.

Name:_____.

Place and date of birth:_____.

Interesting facts, traits, or stories:_____

_____

_____

_____

_____.

Place a photo of your grandparents here.

Additional information about our grandparents:_____

_____

_____

_____

_____

_____

_____

_____

_____

_____.

Our Parents

Children may not know as much as they think they do about their parents. Answers to a few questions can be enlightening, and they can serve as a starting point for long talks that bring generations even closer. Record some of what you've learned below.

MOTHERS' PROFILES:

Name: _____.

Place and date of birth: _____.

Interesting facts, traits, or stories: _____

_____

_____

_____

Name: _____.

Place and date of birth: _____.

Interesting facts, traits, or stories: _____

_____

_____

_____

Place a photo of your parents here.

FATHERS' PROFILES:

Name: _____.

Place and date of birth: _____.

Interesting facts, traits, or stories: _____

_____

_____

_____.

Name: _____.

Place and date of birth: _____.

Interesting facts, traits, or stories: _____

_____

_____

_____.

Additional information about our parents: _____

_____

_____

_____

_____

_____

_____

_____

_____

_____

_____

_____

_____

_____

                              _____

_____

_____

_____

_____

Place a photo of your parents here.

_____

_____

_____

_____

_____

_____

_____ .

Our Generation

*Keeping up with brothers, sisters, and other members of the current generation can be almost as challenging as researching your family history.
Recording a few important facts ensures that the information will be at your fingertips—
and that the next generation won't have to search for it.*

A LITTLE ABOUT US:

Name:_____.

Place and date of birth: _____.

Interesting facts, traits, or stories: _____

_____

_____

_____.

Name:_____.

Place and date of birth: _____.

Interesting facts, traits, or stories: _____

_____

_____

_____.

Our brothers and sisters, and some information about them: _____

_____

_____

_____

_____

_____.

Our cousins, and some information about them: _____

_____

_____

_____

_____

_____.

Ways we keep in touch: _____

_____

_____

_____.

Our legacy for the generations to come is:_____

_____

_____

_____

_____

_____.

Place a photo of family members in your generation here.

Additional information about people in our generation: _____

_____

_____

_____

_____

_____

_____

The Next Generation

The arrival of each new family member brings hope, joy, and dreams.
Even as you look to your family's past, it's equally important to celebrate the future.
In the spaces below, reflect on the younger generation and what you'd like them to know.

The newest member of our family is:

Name _____ Birth Date _____

Other members of the next generation:

Name _____ Birth Date _____

Name _____ Birth Date _____

Name _____ Birth Date _____

Name _____ Birth Date _____

Name _____ Birth Date _____

Name _____ Birth Date _____

Name _____ Birth Date _____

Name _____ Birth Date _____

Name _____ Birth Date _____

Name _____ Birth Date _____

Someday, when _____ is able to read this book, we'd like

them to remember _____

_____

_____.

Other information about the younger generation: _____

_____

_____

_____

_____

_____

_____

_____

_____

_____

_____

_____

_____

_____

_____.

Branching Out

Relatives move away, and, despite everyone's best intentions, branches of a family lose touch. Old letters, newspapers, and phone books can offer valuable clues in your effort to find these family members. Chances are, they might be looking for you, too!

Little is known about the _____ branch of the family.

According to family records or stories, they _____

_____

_____

_____

_____.

Our search turned up the following: _____

_____

_____

_____

_____

_____

_____

_____

_____.

Other relatives we want to learn more about, and what we know about them: _____

_____

_____

_____

_____

_____

_____

_____

_____

_____

_____

_____

_____

_____

_____

_____

_____

_____

_____.

Heirlooms and Keepsakes

The significance of some family treasures—a diamond engagement ring or a carefully drawn portrait—can be easy to see. But other keepsakes may take some investigation: the box of old coins that turns out to be a long-forgotten collection or the seemingly plain frock that you discover was worn as a wedding dress. We value these heirlooms most because they were important to members of our family.

Some treasured family heirlooms:

_____ Origin: _____

_____ Origin: _____

_____ Origin: _____

_____ Origin: _____

_____ Origin: _____

_____ Origin: _____

Our most valuable heirloom in dollars is _____

_____

_____.

A piece with priceless sentimental value is _____

_____

_____.

_____ gets credit for saving many of these family heirlooms.

Our family's most unusual keepsake is_____

_____

_____.

The possession of ours that I hope the next generation will treasure is_____

_____

_____.

Other information about family heirlooms and keepsakes: _____

_____

_____

_____

_____

_____

_____

_____

_____

_____

_____

_____.

Holiday Memories

*Families and their traditions, some handed down for generations,
mean more than expensive gifts or elaborate decorations.
Below, record some memories and traditions that are important to your
family's holiday celebrations.*

The holiday(s) most important to our family: _____

_____

_____.

One of our longest-held traditions is _____

_____

_____.

It wouldn't be _____ in our family without

_____.

A holiday tradition unique to our family is _____

_____

_____.

This tradition was started by _____

_____

_____

_____.

Foods help make the holidays special. Some of our holiday favorites include: _____

_____

_____

_____.

Other holiday memories and traditions:_____

_____

_____

_____

_____

_____

_____

_____

_____

_____

_____

_____

_____

_____

Place a holiday photo here.

_____

_____

_____

_____

_____

_____

_____ .

Family Recipes

Many families say "I love you" with favorite treats, and celebrate with special dishes.
These culinary traditions soon become cherished legacies.
Recording treasured recipes, along with memories of times when those foods were served,
will ensure that those special treats are enjoyed for generations to come!

_____ is a favorite with our family.

Here's the recipe: _____

_____

_____

_____

_____

_____

_____

_____.

This version came from _____

_____

The origin of this tradition seems to be _____

_____

_____.

Other favorite recipes: _____

_____

_____

_____

_____

_____

_____

_____

_____

_____

_____

_____

_____

_____

_____

_____

_____

_____

_____.

Our Traditions

If possible, close families don't wait for holidays and special occasions to get together. Other gatherings can be just as important—whether it's regular Sunday dinner or an annual trip to a beloved location. Times, places, or activities can all hold special meanings when they become imbued with tradition.

A favorite annual get-together is _____

_____.

This tradition originated with _____

_____

_____.

The favorite activity at these gatherings is _____

_____.

_____ is always the life of the party.

Other family traditions: _____

_____

_____

_____

Wedding Bells

Families join together, along with the bride and groom, when marriage vows are exchanged. These unions create new family bonds and strengthen existing ties. Marriage records hold a wealth of information for family tree researchers. Make note of special weddings below.

The most significant marriage records we uncovered document the union of

_____ and _____.

Date: _____ Place: _____

What we know about this pair is _____

_____

_____

_____.

Our family's special wedding traditions include: _____

_____

_____

_____

_____.

Place a wedding photo here.

Other notable weddings: _____

_____

_____

_____

_____

_____

_____ .

Celebrations

Families count on each other to mark special occasions,
whether it's throwing a birthday bash or holding a baby shower.
Individual traditions make these celebrations unique, and even more meaningful.
How does your family celebrate?

Our family birthday traditions call for _____

_____

_____

_____.

Our family never fails to celebrate _____

_____.

Unique traditions associated with these celebrations include: _____

_____

_____.

As far as we know, the oldest celebratory tradition in our family is_____

_____

_____

This originated_____

_____

The best family party organizer is _____.

Other memorable celebrations in our family: _____

_____

_____

_____

_____

_____

_____

_____

_____

_____

_____

_____

_____

_____

_____

_____

_____

_____

_____ .

Family Firsts

Marking beginnings and celebrating achievement remains one of the family's most important roles. These occasions hold meaning not just for the moment but for generations to come.

A "first" that our generation celebrated: _____

_____.

Some past "firsts" and/or achievements that meant a lot to the family include: _____

_____

_____

_____.

Some recent important "firsts": _____

_____

_____

_____.

Educational achievements:_____

_____

_____.

Professional achievements:_____

_____

_____.

Other family "firsts" and how they were celebrated: _____

_____

_____

_____

_____

_____

_____

_____

_____

_____

_____

_____

_____

_____

_____

_____

_____

_____ .

Honorable Mentions

Awards bring honor and pride to the whole family for generations to come.
One of the joys of researching your family tree is discovering outstanding individuals
and their achievements. Record those finds here so that future generations can
also celebrate these distinctions.

Recent accolades accorded to family members include: _____

_____

_____.

An honor uncovered in our family tree search was_____

_____

_____.

The story behind this achievement: _____

_____

_____

_____.

Some outstanding family members, past and present, and their distinctions include: _____

_____

_____

_____

_____

Telling Tales

Delving into your family's past, you're sure to discover colorful characters and varied stories you just can't wait to record. Details may be sketchy, but it's important to keep the stories—and the memories they produce—alive.

One of our favorite family stories is _____

_____

_____

_____

_____.

We first heard this tale from _____.

Truth can be relative. When it comes to this story, we think_____

_____.

Every family has its share of characters. One of our most notable was _____

_____.

The most often-repeated story about her/him is _____

_____

_____

_____

_____

_____.

Other family characters and tales: _____

_____

_____

_____

_____

_____

_____

_____

_____

_____

_____

_____

_____

_____

_____

_____

_____

The Family Business

Trades and professions seem to run in some families just as eye and hair color do in others. Maybe you're the latest in a line of super salespeople or just one more family member dedicated to helping others. Knowing the routes that past generations have followed can help younger family members successfully choose their paths.

The trade/profession that seems to run in our family is _____

_____.

The first family member known to ply this trade was _____

_____.

He/she worked _____(where).

We learned of him/her through _____

_____.

The latest person to take up the "family business" is _____

What they do and where they work: _____

_____

_____.

Other professions or trades in which our family has succeeded: _____

_____

_____

_____

_____

_____

_____

_____

_____.

Place a photo here of a family member at work.

Gifts and Talents

*Legacies don't just take the form of property and bank accounts.
An ear for music, a deft touch with a paintbrush, wizardry in the kitchen,
or countless other talents can be some of the most valuable gifts
that pass from generation to generation.*

Our family talents include _____

_____

_____.

These abilities showed up as far back as _____

_____.

Some especially talented family members and what they're skilled at: _____

_____

_____

_____

_____

_____.

A talent for _____ has shown up only occasionally.

The most unusual talent to appear in our family was _____

_____

_____.

Other family members and their notable talents: _____

_____

_____

_____

_____

_____

_____

_____

_____

_____

_____

_____

_____

_____

_____

_____

_____

_____

_____.

Beloved Pets

Dogs, cats, and other animals play important roles in the family, too.
The record of your family's history wouldn't be complete without their stories.
Below, record information and memories about those "other" beloved family members.

When it comes to pets, our family are _____ lovers.

If there's one pet that stands out in our family past, it's _____ ,

because _____

_____ .

In the present, _____ is an important part of the family.

One of our family's favorite pet stories is _____

_____

_____ .

Other beloved pets our family has owned: _____

_____

_____

_____

_____

_____

_____

_____

Place a photo of a family pet here.

_____

_____

_____

_____

_____

_____

_____

_____

_____.

Hobbies and Pastimes

A love of baseball might run so deep in a family that it seems genetic.
Another clan might produce die-hard fishermen, world-class quilters, or avid readers.
No matter what your family's hobbies might be, these pastimes make up
an important part of who you are.

A favorite pastime in our family is _____

_____.

As far as we know, this hobby started with _____

_____

_____.

Some keepsakes that relate to this hobby include: _____

_____

_____.

Other pastimes our family enjoys: _____

_____

_____

_____

_____

_____

_____

Family Mysteries

Unanswered questions dangle from most family trees.
Maybe there's uncertainty about the family's origins or unknown reasons for
major events. In the course of researching your family history,
you might solve these puzzles—or at least uncover some missing pieces.

One of our family mysteries revolves around _____

_____.

All we know about this question is_____

_____.

The missing piece to this puzzle seems to be _____

_____.

One mystery that we managed to solve is _____

_____

_____.

We found answers by _____

_____.

Other family mysteries, as well as any clues, questions, or theories: _____

_____

_____

_____

It's All in the Family

Bits of humor and wisdom can be priceless family legacies.
Maybe there's a saying that's been handed from father to son or a joke that
has helped in hard times. Record those wise and witty sayings here so that
future generations can appreciate them, too.

One saying I have often heard repeated by family members is _____

_____.

The anecdote that always makes us laugh is _____

_____

_____

_____.

This family joke originated with _____.

Other words of wisdom:_____

_____

_____

_____

_____

_____

_____

_____.

Other jokes or humorous stories: _____

_____

_____

_____

_____

_____

_____

_____

_____

_____

_____

_____

_____

_____

_____

_____

_____

_____.

Setbacks and Challenges

*Families can emerge from hard times stronger than ever.
Stories of challenges met and setbacks overcome serve as examples and
inspirations for future generations.*

One of the greatest challenges our family has faced is _____

_____

_____

_____.

Family members handled this difficulty by _____

_____

_____

_____.

Hardship taught the family _____

_____

_____.

Other challenges, and how the family handled them: _____

_____

_____

_____

Let the Good Times Roll

*Episodes when hard work and hope finally pay off make
the happiest chapters in a family's history. Look closer, and you'll see
that these stories hold deeper messages about perseverance
and believing in each other.*

Hard work paid off in the form of _____

_____ for our family around _____(date).

_____ deserves much of the credit.

It's clear that _____

_____, on the other hand, was mostly a result of luck.

Family members knew their ship had come in when _____

_____

_____.

Other instances of good fortune:_____

_____

_____

_____

_____

_____

_____

Our Heroes

In times of war and other troubles, ordinary people—members of our own families— perform extraordinary deeds. These tales of bravery and endurance deserve to be told again and again.

Family members awarded formal honors include _____

_____

_____.

As told by _____, the story

of _____'s heroism follows:

_____

_____

_____.

Although never recognized formally, _____

_____ has always been admired by the family.

This person qualifies as a true hero because _____

_____.

Place a photo of a family hero here.

Other heroes in our family, and their accomplishments: _____

_____

_____

_____

_____

_____

_____

_____

_____.